My Journey

FAITH UNCOVERED AND LAID BARE

Augustina Samuel

My Journey: Faith Uncovered And Laid Bare

First published in 2013 in the UK by
Third Edition
KESPublishing
London, England

Cover Design: Jonathan Cook

ISBN: 13: 978-0992676858

ISBN: 10: 0992676851

References:
Scriptural quotations used in the book are from the following sources:
Unless otherwise stated all scripture quotations marked 'KJV' **are** taken from the authorized King James Version of the Bible.

Scripture quotations marked 'NIV' are taken from the new International Version of the Bible.

Robert D Putnum and David E Campbell (2010). American Grace: How religion divides and unites us, New York, Simon and Shuster.

James Allen (2007) As a Man Thinketh, Sterling Publishers

Dedicated

To Shaleta, Jamel and Gary, I thank you for your constant belief, support, encouragement, patience and love whilst I undertook this purpose filled task to write this book into existence. I also thank the Lord and all who read My Journey and pray that you are blessed by your encounter.

Preface

The book contains an account of a follower whose journey has intertwined supernaturally with the Bible in various ways. It is an autobiographical study which examines the Self, Spirit and the Flesh. It looks at the importance of the word and scripture. It explores some of the key issues and debate of discourse surrounding the topic of religion i.e. faith, spirituality and consequently discipleship. In order to provide a framework for this discussion, it will explore some of the complex contingencies which surround the discourse relating to religion. For the purpose of this book I will frame the context with the concept of Christianity.

There are three places in the Bible where the term Christian is mentioned: twice in Acts: Acts 11:26 KJV '...and the disciples were called Christian first in Antioch.'
Act 26:28 KJV '...and then Agrippa said onto Paul almost thou persuadest me to be a Christian...' and finally in
1 Peter 4:16 KJV;'...yet if any man suffer as a Christian, let him not be ashamed; but let him glorify God in this behalf...'.

Moreover the Bible shows us that it was others who named disciples as Christians. This was not how they necessarily referred to themselves. This is highlighted as I use the terms disciple and follower interchanging and liberally to provide a context. I acknowledge that I follow the Christian denomination of the Pentecostal faith but rather call myself a student and disciple of Christ following my master, being Gods teachings. Undertaking to do all of this in an attempt to live a full and rewarding spiritual life with meaning that is purpose filled. I mention this as during my early walk I found it a part of my journey to just believe that I was indeed worthy and good enough to hold the title. Upon reflection I believe that this is because, at times faith in contemporary society and the media representations of religion have become stereotyped, loaded and weighed down with negative connotations of what everyone else believes a Christian is. Religion is a politically charged subject and always has been.

Table of content

Introduction

This book is not meant to be a 'How to be a Christian book. It neither claims to tell anyone how to disciple or follow. It is written to give testimony of an account of an 'ordinary' person's journey toward living a Christ like life and the immense impact on that journey the closer I became to the 'Word'. It hopes to demonstrate the fact that it is imperative, that we as Followers read, engage, struggle, run to, be confident in and study the 'Bible'. The power is the word, and the word is the power. The power contained within those pages are of such a magnitude that once you are a believer and you have given your life to the Lord, been saved and baptized, you are able to harness the strength the Bible gives you. It takes on a supernatural, mystical life of its own and the words are no longer just words. I can testify through personal revelation that the Bible is a tool with which the Lord speaks through you, guides you and even chastises you. It is truly amazing. Following and walking in the faith and Spirit demands daily application and a constant vigilance of Self in its Flesh form as it is a continuous journey. Along the road I have learnt to view my mistakes in a new and positive light. Individuals need to view their mistakes as opportunities for us all to learn something different. Just think of how fruitful all of our experiences then become, 'Lessons in Life'. Once we have calmed down and focused away from a flesh response in a particular different situation, we then begin the necessary process in which we attempt to reflect on behaviour, actions and make sense of it all in the Spirit. The only   negative mistakes are the ones where nothing has been learnt. We then call those experiences wasted opportunities for growth as one will end up continually repeating those same mistakes until there is an understanding of why it has occurred and a lesson learnt from that experience.

All of the issues that I have addressed in this book are not used in isolation but with a unifying of the Spirit, thought and guidance which I use and encourage others to use as gentle prompts to aid in gaining a closer more intimate relationship with He whom has made us. The relationship that will be achieved has its own rewards but never to be underestimated are the obstacles that we may face because they are the meat from which we learn. I view my journey metaphorically as the bones and the knowledge gained through the Bible the Holy Ghost Spirit and the love of God as the flesh which are slowly being placed upon my bones which has made me a new being in Christ. The Bible says once we have been reborn we are now in this world, but not of this world. The Parables of the bones in the Old Testament and the book of Ezekiel 37 1-10 offers us a useful way to view the contingencies I highlight. Whilst Ezekiel addresses his dreams the future restoration of Israel he says.

'The hand of the Lord was with me and carried me out in the Spirit of the Lord, and set me down in the valley...full of bones...And he said unto me, Son of Man can these bones live?...I will cause breath to enter into you and ye shall live: And I will lays sinews upon you, and will bring up flesh upon you, and cover you with skin, and put breath in ye, and ye shall live; and ye shall know that I am the Lord'.
Ezekiel 37:1-6

The definition of the word sinew as a noun states that it is:
'A piece of tough fibrous tissue uniting muscle to bone or bone to bone: a tendon or ligament'. This shows that the Lord literally made an army out of dry bones for Ezekiel to carry out his purpose. He made flesh and bone live with the breath of life. He never said as a follower life would be easy. The Bible shows us as followers we are not sheltered from life's trials, test and tribulations. Jesus told us;

'Here on earth you will have many trials.' John 16:33 KJV

In fact as a disciple life will become harder in terms of persecution and ridicule for your belief system. However, the word states, He promised to be with you and bring you calm in the midst of a storm, he does not make mistakes and everything happens for a specific reason. What lesson can I learn from that experience is what we should ask the Lord for guidance with. Albert Einstein said: God doesn't play dice. I believe that every mistake is a unique opportunity to learn something new and push ourself to achieve our goal or ultimate purpose in life. What are we here for? People who do not learn from negative experiences generally continue to make the same mistakes repeatedly until they reflect, respond and analyse what they could have done differently. The Bible shows us how to take responsibility and control of our own actions. It encourages us to have the strength to leave the rest to the Lord he will work it out for us all.

To ascertain, produce and create meaning out of my life. I have learnt that it is necessary to testify the truth upon reflection about why I think I am here and was created. Otherwise life has no meaning. The exploration of my Journey: Faith Uncovered and Laid Bare could only have been made with honesty, humility, scars, flaws and all.

Early Beginnings

From the very moment I had come to know God I realised I just could not turn back.

'Greater is he that is in me than he that this in the world'
1 John 4:4 KJV

My life has been forever changed. However, it is hard due to circumstances and weaknesses of the flesh and the fact that we are living in this world. Thus from time to time we may find ourselves veering away from the Lord and the word. We are then left open. When we look ahead we find that He never changes and He is always right there, where we left him with the same message of repentance, mercy, forgiveness, hope, love and obedience.

'No one who drinks the water I give will ever be thirsty again...'
John 4:14 KJV

Within these pages and the sequel: The Scars and Flaws, I will explore my continual search, journey, battles and struggles in and towards living a Christ-like life. I analyse my interpretation and my way of understanding what it is to be Christ like as I grow in my faith journey and knowledge and so strengthen my relationship with Our Father as I seek intimacy with Our Lord as His child. The Lords Prayer says: '...Our Father which art in Heaven, Hallowed be thy name, Thy Kingdom come, Thy will be done on earth as it is in Heaven'...
Matthew 6:9-13 KJV

Thus when Jesus told us how to pray to God in his Sermon on the Mount. He did not say our will be done, it is Gods will that needs to be done and not our own. Lean not on your own understanding but the Lord's.

As you turn the pages and critically analyse the issues I highlight which I have struggled with and encountered as a

'Babe in Christ' Matthew 18:3-5 KJV, you to will go on your own unique journey into your Spirit and Soul, as a follower or just a Spiritual Being. I have written this book to encourage everyone and spread the good news about the literal power present within the Bible and the importance of feeding ones spiritual life with the words and the attempted application of those words. In so doing provide substance for thy soul. That application has placed the knowledge for us as newborn babes, to desire the sincere love of the word. I pray that whilst you interact you may grow, thereby support others in their Spiritual growth, journey and understanding of His purpose for us all and the realisation of that. We are all called to do one thing which is to save souls, lead others to Christ and spread the word.

'Before I formed thee in the belly, I knew thee, and before thou camest forth out of the womb I sanctioned thee and I ordained thee a prophet unto the nations.'
Jeremiah: 1:5 KJV

The Lord gave me a task over 15 years ago which unbeknown to me began with an idea of writing a book. I studied and prayed for years into my purpose, what it was to be and how I was to obtain it, diligently and although it took years of dedication slowly piece by piece over the years a part of it has come together and it is Kreative Educational Solutions and my sister organisation KESPublishing. Poetic Voices: Voices From The Community, the book which preceded this publication: and My Journey to Discovery written by a colleague. I had a passion for writing and I felt it needed to be explored. I wanted to learn the particular conventions which governed the whole industry of authorship. I went to university to basically learn how to write creatively and perfect my chosen expressive art form. However through persistent prayer, application and battling, passion turned out to be purpose filled. A purpose which took on a life of its own with its own meaning, rewards and fulfilment attached.

I believe that this book has been God generated, informed and sent by Him, whom I thank and give all the praise and glory to for guiding my hands, Mind, Spirit and Soul to have the confidence to give an account of my testimony and study, scars, flaws and all, In the name of Jesus. Everyone needs examples of how other people have achieved whatever state it is that they seek. For all ideologies and theories have differing and opposing views and interpretations of ways of 'understandings' to feed our walk and thus a season within each of our journeys. I am not instructing you on 'how to be' rather informing you of the ingredients necessary. In order to have your own individual unique walk with the Spirit and journey towards Christ.

The Bible

The Bible was written over 2700 years ago. It has been translated and modified by successive generations for clarity, relevance and sharpness of understanding. The Bible began with the The Ten Commandments. It is the most read and biggest, best selling book of all time. It is factual not fictional or a myth. It is the only book that will never be obsolete. UBS World Report 2002 studies into translations of the Bible in various languages and dialects states that the Bible has been translated into 2,287 languages and dialects. Translated out of original tongues diligently, compared and revised. There are various version such as King James and New International among others.

Mark writes '...And the gospel must first be published among all nations...'
Mark 13:10 KJV

It is separated into two sections these are the New and the Old Testaments. There are 66 books in the entire Bible. The shortest verse in the bible is found in John 11:35 KJV 'Jesus wept', this was regarding Martha, Mary and their brother Lazarus. This description shows Jesus's evident compassion. Scripture says, '...Jesus ...saw her weeping and the Jews that came with her, he groaned in the Spirit and was troubled'. John 11:33 KJV The significance of this statement is that it is so powerful when Jesus cries that there is no need for any other words to precede that statement or to follow it. It is a sentence which grammatically stands alone. The magnitude of the fact is enough to know that 'Jesus wept'.

The Old Testament is the Jewish Scriptures i.e. it is considered to be sacred by believers of the Jewish faith and these are the laws which they live by and adopt. It is written in Hebrew and Aramaic, it has 39 books which include: The Creation Story, the books of the Law known as the Torah. The Ten Commandments, Ancient Israel and its various histories, prophecies, and the Psalms. The Psalms are a series of poems, prayers and songs, they are the most well known of all the books of the Bible. The authors are as follows: King David wrote 73, Moses wrote 1 which is Psalm 90 and 49 are written by unknown authors. There are 12 written by Asaph, 12 by The Son's of Korah, Ethan wrote 1 and 2 were written by Solomon. The longest verse in the Bible Is Psalms 119 it is also in the middle of the Bible. Most of the Psalms were penned in Jerusalem. The time frame of when the Psalms were written starts in the 11th Century BC apart from Psalms 90 which Moses penned in the 15th Century BC.

The New Testament is specifically the Christian part of the Bible and is the most read. It is the section of the Bible that we as Christians in contemporary society follow, adopt its guidance and its teachings. It is important to learn lessons from the Old Testament but live in the New Testament. It is written in Greek in the 1st Century AD. The New testament has 27 books including the 4 books of the Gospels written by four of the apostles who are Matthew, Mark, Luke and John. It contains the Acts of the Apostles. They contain descriptions of the early years of Christianity. There are 13 Letters by Saint Paul in which he gives advice about how to live a Christian Life. There are also 8 letters by other early Christian Leaders. There is an apocalyptic vision with the Revelations of Saint John. Luke's are called the Synoptic Gospels as they are very similar to the stories of Jesus. John portrays Jesus in a very different way. The word 'Gospel' means 'good news' and the gospel tells of the good news about Jesus Christ. The new

testament shows the life and ultimate death of Jesus Christ. Peter said '...The word of the Lord stands forever'
Peter 1:25 KJV

Former UK: Prime Minister William Gladstone said "...There is but one question of the hour, how to bring the truths of God's word into vital contact with minds and hearts of all classes..."

Former USA: President Woodrow Wilson said "...A man has deprived himself of this knowledge of the Bible. When you have read the Bible you will know it is the word of God because you would have found it a key to your own heart, your own happiness and your own duty..."

Former USA: President Abraham Lincoln said "...On the Bible I only have this to say that is it is the best gift God has given to man, like the law of gravity..."

William Gladstone's life was transformed by God, Abraham Lincoln tells us that the day he delivered his famous addressed he too, was born again of God's Spirit. Woodrow Wilson also religious and spirit filled.

'...Believe on the Lord Jesus Christ and you will be saved...'
Acts 16:31 KJV

Chapter One

My Journey

My Journey

I believe that everyone of us at some point in our lives will be in pursuit of happiness contentment and fulfilment. Every individual would love to know the meaning of life. The why are we here question? A purpose driven life is based on understanding that there is a higher authority not in this world which we all need to come in submission and agreement with to surrender. I have found that any mention of purpose must include God. Paul addresses this in Colossians when he writes to the Colosse church where heresy had arisen. He asserts the sufficiency of Christ is enough.

'...For by him were all things created, that are in Heaven and Earth, everything, visible and invisible...'
Colossians: 1:16 KJV
'...Everything got started in Him and finds it's purpose in him...'
Colossians: 1:16 KJV
Solomon tells us in Proverbs:
'...A life devoted to things is a dead life, a stump; a God shaped life is a flourishing tree...'
Proverbs: 11:28 KJV

I grew up in a strict religious West Indian, east end home, my parents were born in Dominica, located in the Caribbean but they came to England in 1954 and settled here. They both came from large families and it would appear that is what they planned to have with my siblings and I all nine of us six girls and three boys of which I was the last in the line and legacy. We were brought up Seventh Day Adventist and that was surely how we lived. This was at times hard for me growing up in the 1970s and early 1980s as a child that meant that there was no television on a Saturday as that is The Sabbath Day and Sunday School in addition to Bible studies everyday after school before house chores and duties. Before Sunday School most of us children literally spent all our collection money on sweets as the parents trusted us children, totally unaware where the money really went, because on Sundays, parents stayed home. I always seemed to have a conscience, just that I did not always follow it. I put half of my money in the collection and only spent half on sweets. Around 12 years old I decided there was no other way and as soon as possible I would follow my siblings footsteps. I awaited for my fifteenth birthday when in my family traditionally we were given the choice to continue attending church or stay home.

Looking back there was definitely a breakdown in communication with a lot of my peers and our parents and I was no different as it seemed that they did not understand or even comprehend the identity crisis we were all experiencing. I believe that this was due to a general lack of understanding from our parents and a lack of cultural understanding in the educational system. Not to mention that this was all characterised with the onslaught of adolescence which served no purpose it seemed. Thus although religion framed my early childhood experiences and psyche, values, morals and social conscience, I later grew to resent it through out my teenage and early adult years. I made every effort to run from it and resist my parents discipline and guidance as soon as I was able to.

We were never destitute as my father always worked as a master builder. I always remember as a child when we would go for our 'regular Sunday drives' to visit our family dotted across London. My father felt that our visits kept us in contact with family and provided an inexpensive day out for the family. Driving through the City of Westminster he would always say the same thing. "All you children, in a broad Dominican accent I built this bank, I built that office", as though we had never heard it before and it was new information. Back then I believed my father built Bank, West-End and the whole of London, for that matter. He later went to work in the Ford Dagenham Car Plant.

Our standard of life growing up could not exactly be described as the Dickensian character of 'Oliver Twist'! poor but I always wore 'hand me downs'. Apart from my Sunday best that was my 'good clothes' and only for church and going out. On occasions it seemed that it was not the greatest thing having five sisters preceding me in regards to clothes as it was difficult for my parents to justify buying me new clothes when my sisters had out grown their old clothes and there was a mortgage to be paid for. We always had lodgers renting rooms which was common place in those days as it provided an extra source of income for families. We had the Rag and Bone Man based at the top of our road in the alleyway between St Georges Square and St Georges Road. The alleyway had a cobbled floor I liked the sound of the horses hoofs as they clattered on the floor when they strode along. There were several stables adjoining to it which housed the horses that pulled the carts. There where sections for coal, chestnut roasting all sorts seemed to go on there as a child it was quiet exciting to me.

I never knew the Rag and Bone Mans name but he had a dirty well worn face he wore a cap and had a memorable traditional cockney accent. He was a typical East-ender. He would ride his horse and cart down our street, ring his bell and shout "any ole rags, any ole rags, any ole rags for sale ladies". All of the mothers would then come out of their houses and trade clothes they had for others or bought alternatives in the middle of the street. The whole thing was like a portable market that only last 15 minutes. He also sold coal for our fires which he delivered once a week into our coal seller through the manhole outside our front door. Funny, because I never saw him get paid. In those days my mother always 'ticked or trusted' a lot of Working Class people where I grew up did that back then. Mama would 'trust' everyday produce like milk, eggs, bread and juice from the milkman. Meat from the butchers or groceries from the corner shop and buy them a present for Christmas and give them some money. This just meant buy now and pay later, usually at the end of the month on my fathers pay day. Upon reflection I consider myself privileged and it to be an advantage to have grown up in the era and time period that I did. It gave me a strong sense of self and helped me to develop character, taught me to take responsibility, problem solve and more importantly resilience with the knowledge and introduction to God through the word and the values and morals which were instilled. When I was first saved I would reflect on my upbringing in Christ and my interaction with the Bible and not be able to understand why I could not really remember the scriptures which had shaped my early formation of 'being'. I would ponder on why I did not know of or even understand it. Now that I am on my journey I read the words and they have resonance for me. I understand the concept of salvation, mercy, repentance and forgiveness as a living organism and state of being in Christ. The Bible is an extraordinary book. I have read studied re-read and continue to read and study the Bible yet each time I interact with it I discover and learn to see and understand the biblical narratives and their meanings in new and improved ways. I will study and read it until I pass away and still find new ways. I will be a scholar until the end as learning is life long and always will be.

The Light

The Light

Around 1976 one of my brothers returned home from his all white boarding school in Chelmsford for good, where he attended for four years. However he was different. He refused to comb his hair and said he was a Rastafarian, I believe as his response to the anti-establishment occurring from disaffected youths of the day. It was a time when links were being rediscovered in regards to racial identity and the Pan African Movement was being established. He was around sixteen or so and was experiencing adolescence and searching for his own identity and place in society. This was much to my parents dismay they just did not understand in their eyes his deliberate disobedience as they saw it. He began to smoke Marijuana and refused to eat chicken or meat. He was in essence a Vegan. I remember he stopped using salt, pepper or any kind of seasoning for that matter and ate a mainly vegetables. He insisted on following the Rastafarian teachings that worshipped Haile Salassie I as a prophet. They also adopted some of the ways of a group called the Nazarite's which is detailed in Numbers which states:

'...No razor shall come onto his head until the days be fulfilled....and shall let the locks of the hair of his head grow...'
Numbers 6:4-5 KJV

I was eight years old and I would secretly creep up the stair to the fourth floor of our house and his attic room to listen at his bedroom door and I would hear him and friends speaking. They began to interpret the Bible in totally different ways which sounded a lot more interesting than Mama and Daddy but some what unconventional and more radical than what I had known or heard of. My parents never discussed race in the terms that they did. My parents just told us that "Some people don't like Black people", and should just be ignored that was that. Racism was a concept but not a term that was really used. Racism was not a word in our vocabulary back then, it was just portrayed as a part of the territory. The situation became intolerable for my parents they even offered him £100.00 pounds to cut his locks off. He refused of course so they went in on him one night like an undercover covert operation, blankets and all and attempted to hold him down and cut them off in his sleep. The result was he clung to them even more. He would listen to the genre of reggae music called 'Culture' which seemed quite radical but documented the 'black experience.' They had radical names like Burning Spear, Steel Pulse, Culture, Black Uhuru meaning freedom, Linton Kwasi Johnson a UK based political dub poet who emerged in the 1970's and 1980's, as well as Bob Marley who my brother would visit in the Savoy Hotel and stay with him when he was in the country. In those days Bob was very approachable. Ironically some years later in the 1980's, my brother asked my oldest sister to cut his locks off and he put them in a carrier bag and that was it. He never told us why he finally cut them off but he moved to the Isle of Wight where he lived for over 20 years and even had all of his children which reside there. It seemed that the system that made him grow his locks was also responsible for him finally cutting them off.

The 1970's was an era marred with technological advancements, change, civil disobedience, challenging of authority, the 'norm' and the status quo. On many fronts people were seeking liberating ways to live. Anti establishment formed the backdrop to my childhood. Ordinary people all over the world were on the march. There were protest against the Vietnam War, equalities i.e. feminist challenging gender roles, the rise of gay rights and sexual liberation or sex without responsibility, disabilities to racial conflict it was altogether a liberating but explosive era in history.

To Mama with Love

Mama had me in 1967 at the age of 47 years old in the middle of her Menopause. She had my sister aged 42 years old and lost a set of twins aged 44 years old that hurt her as she was a twin and came from a family of six sets of twins. She had diabetes and high blood pressure thus she was advised by the doctors to abort the fetus as it had become legal for married women that year. My parents were told that I would be born as a Spastic the awful name given at the time, the disability is now known as Down Syndrome. My parents were advised that Mama could also die during childbirth. I was told that they said that they were God fearing people and they will leave it in the hands of the Lord. I was born fit and healthy but the stress was too much for her body. She had to be given a hysterectomy directly after she gave birth to me as she had a "drop womb" as she referred to it. I was always with her not out of choice but my other siblings were older teenagers doing their own thing and they certainly did not want to be around Mama as expected or me their annoying little sister as they saw it. I was never the same as or even close to my siblings growing up partly because of the age gap and partly due to the fact that they were always bullying me as I was the youngest and in their minds and spoilt. I was short, little and fairer than all my other siblings. I looked so different to everyone else that even strangers would comment. Thus eventually "Your the milkman's child", became a running joke in the family. For years their cruel jibes actually caused me to questioned my parentage. However, as the milkman was caucasian I always knew that they were just being unkind. Nevertheless it highlighted the fact that I was certainly different to my other siblings very early on in my life.

She always spoke in parables about life lessons about her up bringing and past life in Dominica before coming to England with pure fondness and nostalgia and she relished repeating her stories enthusiastically. I loved hearing the stories but they were full of morality the images and memories are still vivid of Mama and her story telling. It was an everyday activity carried out as she cooked for us I listened as she cleaned and marinated the meat or chicken along with the washing of the rice and boiling the Congo Peas. She was always busy, with such a big family to care for. Sunday mornings I would wake to Mama banging the pots in the kitchen as she cooked and cleaned whilst she sang traditional gospel hymns, "I am coming Lord coming onto thee, wash me cleanse me in that blood that flows from Calvary". Mama spoke to me a lot because I was the youngest and I was always with her. My father was not allowed to discipline me, she felt that he disciplined the rest and it was her turn. I was later told by my cousin and father that my mother described me as her 'Pension'. I was definitely my mothers child in many ways. Consequently, for sometime I was puzzled as to what she meant by the term 'Pension'. Since writing this book I have come to think of Mamas 'Pension' in me as the keeper of the essence of her and her memory. Her thoughts, views, faith in God and of course her stories. She would say things like "When you grow you will know", in her broad Dominican accent. It was as though she knew that she would not be here for my formative years when I would need the comfort and guidance of a loving mother. Mama never ever said that she loved me but she never said things like that, she was brought up to show it. She always believed, "Actions speak louder than words". I would have still loved to have heard the words and endeavour to say it to my children regularly. Thus she sowed seeds of knowledge, advice and guidance for me to pick up when I had the spiritual wisdom and life's maturity to understand and to use them within my life.

My parents ruled the home with the rod of discipline in one hand and the Bible in the other. We grew up with the knowledge that there was a scripture for everything, situation and occasion and that was drummed into us. It would be "Pick up that piece of rubbish child, cleanliness is next to Godliness or during disciplining "spare the rod and spoil the child" as I was being chastised. I say that but this was normal behaviour in most caribbean homes at that time so it never seemed that bad. In hindsight that, which caused me to run from God strangely drew me near and helped me find my way home. It is always important to sow seeds in Christ, meaning values, morals, right and wrong in your children. Even when I did what was not correct behaviour in Christ, I understood that it was wrong. I just choose not to heed. However, through my life and work I have seen how sad it is when an individual has no spiritual grounding at all and no idea or concept of what is wrong in Christ to start with. There is then the need to learn new ways never really thought of previously, thought processes will need adjustment or radical re-thinking. It was that foundation and instilling of Christian values, morals that acted as a beacon which lit the way home for me when it was the correct time for my journey to be resumed.

My mother had a stroke in October 1994 which left her in a deep comatose state. She never spoke or even ate. It seemed as though she had a tube for everything coming out of every orifice and that was hard to watch at 27 years old that is when it began. All of us siblings were forced to watch my mother lay there. It felt like she had become a frozen corpse and I felt that a paraplegic was in a far better state than her because at the very least they were lucid and coherent and could express share through various technical means available. Thus, still love and acknowledge your presence. However I did not acknowledge the issue of quality of life as I was an emotional wreck and irrational. That was a very difficult period and it felt like a dark shadow hung over my life. We were left just waiting for her to pass. The doctors first told us that she would not live to see Christmas 1994. She defied that prediction and their specialist advice. We could not agree with authorities about her care and where she would be moved to. She had been in Newham General for one year. She was in a private room and It was winter but whenever we went to see our mother the room was freezing cold and the window was left wide open. This meant that she kept catching pneumonia. No one listened to our concerns, thus not wanting to endanger her care, we agreed to bide our time and we kept a constant vigil around her, thank the Lord she had 9 children. I would go and lay on the bed with her cuddle up and speak to her about all the trauma and drama that was happening in the family, even though there was never any response, I felt some

that the image of the church needs to evolve in its approach in contemporary society to be able to relate to all individuals, unsaved and the world but more importantly the youth as they are our future for tomorrow. In today's society the church is regularly criticised for being hypocritical because society has an old fashioned stereotypical image of what a Christian actually looks and sounds like. Consequently if an individual does not fit into the 'stereotypical Christian framework of reference' new and established disciples are made to feel intimidated by believers and non-believers alike because of their own lack of belief and misunderstanding of Christ and the Bible.

It feels as though there is need of a radical shake up and overhaul in some of our christian churches in modern day society to be more inclusive of differences in others, just as when Christ came to teach us. We need to welcome new ways of reaching out, that does not contaminate the Bible and its doctrines. We must never forget what we are actually here for a time and purpose. Modern society has seen the Christian network harnessing media to reach out to others and spread the word. Television Evangelism, the Internet, social media, social mediums are all ways we have expanded. The traditional more regimented forms of worship and praise has its place but there is alway room for new ways of learning, expressing and seeing things differently. We have an issue with Christians moving from church to church as they have experienced politics of the flesh. Moving around in churches from church to church can paralyse us in our journey and stunt our spiritual growth until we settle. If we are not happy with the church we attend we must pray continually for a solution before we leave as we will find ourself moving from church to church bringing the issues with us. I have learnt to always try to look at what I could do to change the situation, is there a ministry which is lacking or an issue in the church which needs addressing which the Lord wants us to bring to the forefront?. Or is it just us operating in the flesh or others treating us in the flesh?. Unless you feel that the Lord wants you to leave stay put and work it out. It is important to note that it may just simply be that you know that the Lord wants you to move as I have come to learn. The security of the spirit of a church unit is essential. If you are a disciple there must be someone leading such as a Pastor and Senior Pastoral Team. I am well aware that it does not always work like that and I myself have felt like a forgotten soldier within my church also at times. However, I always try to remember Gods work is bigger than any flesh and I stay focused with my eyes on my purpose. Obedience is the key it is necessary for purpose fulfilment to occur. The Children of Israel are typical examples of what happens when you do not listen. Obey and submit to those that are over you. The Bible says:

'Peter therefore was kept in prison: but prayer was made without ceasing of the church unto God for him': This shows the power of collective prayer as a church and body in Christ.
Churches are run as businesses or it would be impossible to open the doors every Sunday let alone undertake the missionary work of many Christians. There are people who need to be paid for the work that they carry out. However, lets be mindful that we do not make the Fathers House into a den of thieves and too commercialised. When Jesus went to Jerusalem and entered into the temple. 'He cast out all them that sold and bought into the temple, and overthrew the tables for the moneychangers, and the seats of them that sold Doves. .Jesus said: "...It is written, My house shall be a house of prayer; but ye have made it a den of thieves..."
Matthew 21:12–13 KJV

The church, its doctrine and Christ is just as relevant in our lives today as He has always been, even more so as Revelations could be suggested as confirming the fact that we are living in the last days one has just to look at all of the examples of modern day conflicts in the Middle East and Africa as well as right here with Ireland and world disasters in recent years, famine and floods. One has only to watch the news and read the daily newspapers, its all there.

It could be argued that some followers and non-believers in contemporary society could be suggested as promoting the Gospel and the doctrine which it holds and the ideology that surrounds the key issues and debates relating to the concept of 'Christianity', in an old, redundant and unapproachable manner, just as when Christ was sent to teach and save us His children. It has been suggested that to be a Christian you must first live a perfect life, then become baptised and invite him into your life. Baptism is crucial to begin the journey but It is misunderstood for me it was made to appear as though I must first cleanse myself and stop all my bad habits and unclean lifestyle before I came and surrender myself to Christ. In contrast I have learnt that it is, in effect the exact opposite of what He ask. It is impossible to do it alone. You need his help support.

Dividing Religious Issues

Professor Bob Putnam in his book American Grace: How Religion Divides Us, has a useful way to view the contingencies involved: Professor Bob Putnam discusses the topic of how religion has polarised American communities. He analyses a ABC News poll taken that found American white men were the least religious of all ethnicities. However, surprisingly Americans were generally more religiously aware than some countries like Iraq in the Middle East. It also found more division in religious beliefs. He argues the Middle East even Ireland are used as examples of countries experiencing civil religious conflict. It also noted that there were a number of marriages which cross religious lines i.e. Catholics marry Baptist, Muslims marry Christians and so on. It showed that 40% of individuals changed their religious beliefs for a relationships and partner. He discusses the issue of 'Personal Networks' which have bound Americans together which is in contrast tearing their beliefs apart as he asserts that it also causes a divide in their own beliefs. The study found that some Christians believed none Christians can be saved and a good person not of their faith can go to Heaven. However he asserts that from their point of view as an evangelical Christian, these are the the wrong answers.

He referred to a new phenomenon called NONES: The young nones: which basically means No religious affiliation. When surveyed it showed that 33% of young people were alienated from organised religion but they believe not from God. Even though they would not describe themselves as atheist as they believe in God, pray and read the Bible and would have most probably been brought up in religious homes but have misunderstand what religion is.

He asserts, Evangelicals are in the business of saving souls not politics. He argues right wing politics are driving people away from the church. He talks of the new wave of Evangelicals like Rick Warren who takes a different approach to Evangelism. He believes followers are moving away from politics and back to what they know "The business of saving souls for the Lord". Here Warren is seen as a 'poster boy' for the younger generation who are trying to get away from that stereotypical conventional Republican Party image. He says that their right winged political judgmental view of religion is irresponsible and is turning many people away from the church. It appears that there is no space for them and more importantly they do not believe that it includes them. He believes that is a dangerous mix with a price to pay for all in the future. The poll found that there was no variation in levels of alcoholism and divorce in the church as among non believers.

It outlined the rapid growth of churches in the USA it also highlighted an emergence of 'Eclectic Theology'. Here there is an example of traditional beliefs from doctrine totally mis understood. Here we have opposing beliefs and traditional views juxtaposed. There is belief in the resurrection and reincarnation, guidance through prayer and guidance through Horoscopes. The results no fundamental principal and understanding that one can not serve two Gods. We are then attempting to surmise what it means to be a 'Christian' in contemporary society.

The result is that we as individuals tend to forget the good book has advice and guidance on every single matter from business to friendship and family. It shows us that he used murderers, thief's, prostitutes, adulterers and a number of people who would have been seen as unsavoury characters to perform great acts in the biographical stories told of in the Bible. Great men in and biblical testimonies and narratives struggled with their purpose and faith and even fell out of Gods favour at times but repented and were forgiven by the Lord. The Bible tells us that God still loved them. Moses was disobedient so he did not get all that was intended for him. He was shown the promised land that his people would inherit but told he had to leave it to Joshua to lead the people. King David also fell out of favour when he killed Bathsheba's husband Uriah after he impregnated her, then married her. Thus the Lord sent Nathan, allowing King David to pass judgement on himself as his heart had become hard toward the Lord and his people. Things were never easy. However as He is a merciful and forgiving God, King David fasted, prayed and repented for what he had done that was not pleasing to God. The child died, but later it was Bathsheba that bore the son Solomon and that child was greatly favoured by the Lord with the gifts of wisdom and understanding bestowed upon him. He also built the temple to the Lord, foretold and ordained before his birth. This illustrates how good can come out of bad when the Lord touches the situation with forgiveness and mercy. The Bible is full of numerous figures and people that received Gods mercy, grace and gifts through obedience and building a intimate relationship with God and in so doing they realised and performed His purpose for them.

The Lord does not call 'perfect people' to serve Him he calls humble, open people that he can shape, mould and use.

'For ye see your calling brethren how that not many noble are called....'
2 Corinthians: 1:26 KJV

He calls the unworthy the exact opposite of noble. He always calls the most unlikely character to make a difference or perform his ministry. In order for them to testify and bring glory to his name. He continually demonstrates that he can make the unworthy worthy and the impossible possible. It could be described as modern day miracles. The day a man reaches the state of 'perfection' he would have to be called God as He is 'perfection' none other.

The Commandments

'For the Commandments is like a lamp: and the law is light: and reproofs on instruction are the way of life.'
Proverbs 6:23 KJV.

It was 2007 and I was now in the ARC and I once listened to a lead pastor in my church, who preached a sermon about the Ten Commandments. He discussed them in a unique way that I had never thought of previously. He defined them as rules, codes of conduct, a tool to be use to govern, discipline and control our own behaviour. He introduced the idea to me that the commandments are everyday guidelines which we as individuals can strive to obtain to reach a Christ like state. However due to our obvious imperfections as human beings, it may never be achieved in the context of most individuals adhering to all laws at once as handed down by Moses after he had gone up to Mount Sinai to receive Gods law as it is written when God cast his law in stone, The Arc of the Covenant. We all fall short even those of us in Christ, let a lone non believers.

It is correct that all of Gods laws are important. The New Testament shows us that we should all endeavour to live our lives that way at all times. However, even as followers of Christ it is difficult as we are born of sin from the very beginning with Adam and Eve when that first sin was committed. Jesus was sent to reverse that sin and give us grace, salvation and salvation. Consequently, for me there are three main commandments which I have come to believe stand on and stand out for me they are: Love your God and put no other God before me, Love one another as you love yourself and more importantly: do unto others as you would have them do unto you. I have found this to be the key to unlock all for me. Attempting to follow these three simple rules with continual striving and reflecting of correcting fleshly behaviours within myself. I try to be aware of my thoughts and motives in order to be on guard from my own flesh mind and tongue, thus ready to call for help from the Spirit as I act in the Spirit. However, I acknowledge and strive to attain and work towards implementing all of the commandments.

For example: I do not like people lying to me, so I try not to lie to others. I do not like people stealing from me, so I do not steal from others. I want to be blessed and possibly sit at the right hand or anywhere near the Lord that I can in Heaven for eternity. I pray for the Lord to give me a forgiving heart constantly as He exercises forgiveness of me everyday. This is the one that I found the most difficult previously. This has been made much easier in my walk when I have thought about myself and how often I do incorrect things in Christ knowingly and unknowingly and the Father always forgives me. I have not committed murder as obviously who wants to be killed. I want to be loved so I extend love and lovingkindness to others. I knew that I do not forgive for anyone but myself, soul and spirit.

I have learnt the danger of being jealous or envious of what my friends or neighbour or anyone else has. I am always happy for everyone and try to be encouraging, be it a new car, an outfit, might be a job or even someones family. I never forget the fact that I do not know what that person has sacrificed lost or gained to have whatever it is. I am also aware that I am unsure if I would pray whatever the cost is that they have paid to have whatever it may be. Therefore, It is better to be encouraging and supportive to others with their blessings as envy has never been a good look, demeanour or emotion on anyone. Envy is accountable for all manner of wrongs committed in its name so stay away from it at all cost. It is a negative emotion sent from the Devil to entice you, do not give it access. Its remit is to cause confusion, chaos, hatred and devastation. Consequently, that is just what it will bring negativity of the worst kind. I have been blessed enough that God has allowed me to bear fruit and produce heirs and nurture children of my own. Thus, before my parents passed I was taught to treat parents with respect.

"...Honor your father and your mother, so that you may live long..."
Exodus 20:12 KJV

The Lord asks us to honour our parents so that it may go well with us and the legacy of our family to come. Children generally do what they see. Parenthood is one of the lowest paid roles yet it is the most important job which we as individuals will ever undertake with no manual, formal training or qualifications, if we accept the challenge. It is the most overlooked and underestimated role we in society can play in our live span. In my opinion it is selfless, demanding, all sacrificing, and bordering on subtle abuse at times when children are teenagers. However it is still an undertaking which has allowed me to evolve and grow and that I have been blessed for accepting. Parenthood is so not materialistic. In contrast it is an altruistic, engulfing love that can be truly rewarding with unimaginable heights of euphoria and adulation. It is the only way to ensure the continuation of your lineage and blood line. I do not discount adoptive families and parents as the story of Ruth gives us a good effective example of this. Parents are not biological. It is also the nurturer, the person who cleaned up the cuts and grazes or sat up all night sick with worry when illness came. Parenthood has no monetary rewards. Thus respect for our parents is a necessity if we are to hope to become parents in the future. One day I would like my children to do the same. Respect with love and obedience the sacrifices I have made in order to give them life and rare them. Intern I have had to stomach the lost and anguish of suffering from betrayal of a loved one. In my experience it is senseless to have an adulterous affair and ruin lives. Go home and work it out or seek mediation and spiritual guidance. Lies and dishonesty brings more heartache. If it is an impossible situation there should be honesty. That would have stopped a huge amount of unnecessary hurt caused through dishonesty in my previous marriage. Instead as human beings we gravitate to an end where we have created more issues through the distrust which will inevitably build. Exodus 20:2-17 KJV

The Ten Commandments

"You shall have no other Gods before me. You shall not make for yourself an image in the form of anything in Heaven above or on the earth beneath or in the waters below. You shall not bow down to them or worship them; For I, the Lord your God am a jealous God, punishing the children for the sin of the parents to the third and fourth generation of those who hate me, but showing love to a thousand of generations of those who love me and keep my commandments. You shall not misuse the name of the Lord your God, for the Lord will not hold anyone guiltless who misuses his name.

Remember the Sabbath Day by keeping it holy. Six days you shall labor and do all your work, but the seventh day is a sabbath day to the Lord your God. On it you shall do any work, neither you, nor your son or daughter, nor your male or female servants, nor your animals, nor any foreigner residing in your towns. For in six days the Lord made the heavens and the earth, the sea, and all that is in them, but he rested on the seventh day. Therefore the Lord blessed the Sabbath day and made it holy.

"Honor your father and your mother, so that you live long in the land that your God is giving you. You shall not give false testimony against your neighbor. You shall not covet your neighbor's house. You shall not covet your neighbor's wife, or his male or female servant, his ox donkey, or anything that belongs to your neighbor."
Exodus 20:2-17 KJV

Chapter Three

Fellowship

Fellowship

Through Christ your life has meaning as he has a purpose for each and everyone of us created before we were even born. If you choose to follow Him.

"I am your creator, you were in my care even before you were born."
Isaiah 44:2 KJV

"I know you by name. Exodus 33:12

"The Lord has made everything for His own purposes. Proverbs16:4 KJV

To follow as a disciple can be hard but it gives your life meaning and it is always rewarding, empowering and life affirming. Giving is like a spiritual beacon it allows for a continual shower of blessings upon your life and circumstances. Denzil Washington once said during an interview with Oprah Winfrey, "Man will give you the awards in life but the Lord will give you the reward in Heaven", which I believe is eternal and worth more than material wealth when our days are done on this earth. Riches are for a time but you can not take it with you and it is of no use in death apart from funeral cost. Riches can be defined in many ways and the old saying money can not buy you happiness is proven to be true continuously. It is still important to admit that I would be a liar if I did not say that I would rather be financially stable and unhappy as oppose to poor and unhappy as not having the pressure of the lack of finances for living expenses can make my disposition a little more bearable allowing for a plethora of options available to me to ease my pain with the freedom that financial security can bring. Riches are not always based in the material sense necessarily as riches can be defined through being blessed and allowed to parent and be blessed with a child to rare and shape that will continue your legacy and line.

The Bible states:
'Riches are not forever...Lo children are an heritage of the Lord and the fruit of the womb is his reward...As arrows are in the hand of a mighty man so are children of the youth.. Happy is the man that hath his quiver full of them...'
Psalms 127:3-5 KJV

Being rich with material wealth and financial status is not a determinant of who 'gets into Heaven' it does not omit one neither.

The Bible says:
'...For the love of money is the root of evil...'
1 Timothy 6:10

'...He that trust in his riches shall fall: but the righteous shall flourish as a branch...'
Proverbs 1:28 KJV

This illustrate the fact that having money is not bad. Worshipping money is what leads to evil as it is placed above all else. I always find it difficult to understand why one of the most fundamental things we are ask to do as followers is constantly misunderstood or watered down to be more appetising and palatable even to followers. It always has and always will be by our deeds which is how we live our lives. What is your legacy? What have you left to say that you were here? Is what we need to ask ourselves.

'For thou rendereth every man according to his work.'
Psalms 62:12 KJV

What is my God given purpose? What have I done for others and how have I contributed to the kingdom, our deeds. The Bible is very clear on that fact. It is also very clear on the fact that we must repent, be saved, baptised, pray, follow the masters teaching, die and be reborn, leave the old you behind, to find a new improved you as a follower. There you have it, not enough to just, be a 'good person'. Again wealth alone does not mean that you can not be a follower and enter into Heaven. Neither do you gain automatic status for being poor.

'A rich mans wealth is his strong city: the destruction of the poor is their poverty' Proverbs 10:15 KJV

The Bible says, '...It is easier for a camel to go through the eye of a needle, than for a rich man to enter the Kingdom of God...' Matthew 19:24 KJV

'...For we receive the due reward of our deeds...'
Luke: 23:41 KJV

I found these scriptures slightly un-nerving and totally confusing as an early believer. The word shows us continually that it is by our own hands that we bring our final and eternal judgement at the appointed time, through the deeds we do on earth whilst alive. It is all about giving an account of our lives. Some people say what goes around comes around or even call it Karma. I just call it Gods work coming together for the good of His children and His purpose.

'...For we must all appear before the judgement seat of Christ, that everyone may receive the things done in his body, according to that he hath done, whether it be good or bad...'
2 Corinthians 5:10 KJV

'And we know that all things work together for the good to them that love God to them that are called according to purpose'
Roman 8:28 KJV

Prayer

Prayer

There are 168 hours in each week, how many of those hours can you say you devote to prayer, spiritual enrichment, growth and ultimately, intimacy with your Father. That is a point for you to ponder as you interact with the words on these pages.

By strengthening my prayer life I have come to learn there is no need to stand on ceremony and think of what words to use in prayer. During my intimacy with the Lord, I speak and let the Spirit guide my mouth and heart, oh sweet surrender. He hears all my prayers long and short.

The Bible states '...But when you pray use not vain repetitions, as the heathen do: for they think that they shall be heard for much speaking...'
Matthew 6:7 KJV

I speak in the Spirit from my heart and allow the Spirit to give me utterance. I never let the the act of prayer be underestimated. When I pray I learnt to visualise myself transported to a place of intimacy, privacy and quiet. In my spiritual meditative state I go to an island and I imagine I am on a deserted beach. The sea is calm and clear blue. The sky is bright and there is no pollution. I myself am in awe like Mary sitting at Jesus's feet with Martha in the Kitchen cooking. I then speak to him as a child speaks to their father. I ask him for guidance, support and correction. I cry, laugh, and question him, ask for forgiveness and receive, I also listen and ask him to show me his will on many situations or circumstances, then I put it in his hands. I read my Bible minimum four scriptures a day and I take notes, study and discuss the scriptural readings in fellowship with family and friends. For years as an early believer I would have to have a shower clean my room, I had a whole process of personal purification that I went through before I entered my intimate time with God as I thought it disrespectful. But now that I am in a different place I pray as soon as I wake just brush my teeth. I might add that this has only changed this year through spiritual growth. However, I believe that everyone of us have to go through a process while learning how to communicate. The two prayers: A prayer for protection from Ephesians and one of increase Prayer of Jabez .These prayers have been said over my life from 1998 not long after being saved. I now understand fully what they mean and I have spoken the words into my life.

Paul tells us about the need for us as followers to keep ourselves covered and protected with the word and he writes the importance of prayer and putting on and using The armor of God. He states:

These two prayers I am not without, they are a part of my daily covering and attire which cover my Soul and Spirit. I have said these prayers over my life and that of my family for the last fifteen years. Jabez prayed against the life set out for him he was born in pain and that was his title but he prayed for increase and a change in his circumstances. Even when I was not in church I always prayed and I believe that a lot of people do.

Putting on the Armour

'Put on the armour the of God that ye may be able to stand against the wiles of the Devil. For we wrestle not against flesh and blood, but against principalities, against powers, against the rulers of the darkness of this world. Against spiritual wickedness in high places. Wherefore take onto you the whole armour of God, that you may be able to withstand in the evil day, And having done all, to stand. Stand therefore, having your loins girt about with truth, and having on the breastplate of righteousness: And your feet shod with the preparation of the gospel of the peace: Above all, taking the shield of faith wherewith you shall be able to quench, All the fiery darts of the wicked. And take the helmet of salvation and the sword and the Spirit, which is the word of God: Praying always with all prayer and supplication in the Spirit, and watching there onto with all perseverance and supplication for all saints: And

for me, that utterance may be given unto me, that I may open my mouth boldly, to make known the mystery of the Gospel. For which I am an ambassador in bonds: that therein I may speak boldly, as I ought to speak...'
Ephesians 6:10–20 NKJV

The Prayer Of Jabez

'...And Jabez called on the God of Israel, saying, oh that thou wouldest bless me in deed, and enlarge my coast, and that thine hand might be with me, and thou wouldest keep me from evil, that it may not grieve me, and God granted him that which he had requested...'
1 Chronicles 4:10 KJV

Individuals not practicing any faith have still been known to seek the Lord at the end when their existence is about to cease. Before I knew intimacy with God. I regularly fell to my knees and prayed whenever I was lost and believed that no earthly person could help me. When my prayers were answered I would put it down to 'luck' forgetting I did pray so I should thank God and fulfil my agreement, whatever it was at the time. I have found that prayer can really move mountains and make what seems to be impossible and unreal, possible and real. I have often made a promise to perform some act considered to be a 'good deed' or an attempt at living right and try to 'change my ways' and even then he always answered. Consequently, as He is a forgiving God all He ask is that we repent and we shall be forgiven.

I believe that prayer is one of the most powerful acts that one must perform as a disciple as it is through prayer and intercession that we speak to the Lord our Father as His children seeking guidance, love, support, healing and just someone to speak to whom listens, cares and we know has our best interest at heart. In the Old Testament Samuel the last of the Judges described lack or cease from prayer as a sin.

It states:
'...Moreover as for me God forbid that I should sin against the Lord in ceasing to pray...'
1 Samuel 12:23 KJV

Sometimes we forget to actually ask and speak to him about literally everything. In society children automatically ask for whatever they want be it small or large and it is expected of them. In adulthood through socialisation into society 'social norms' dictate that we are conditioned to stop asking for the menial things as an adult we want to do things alone, independently and that is expected. All of this is fine in the flesh but that is dangerous in the Spirit. We have to continually learn to pray for what we need. There is a need to recondition our prayer life to fully include everyday all day constant little chats like a quick email, twitter, texts or even BB's to the Lord. The Lord gives us the most effective example of the most caring and unconditional love of a devoted parent.

The Lord say, '...Pray about everything...tell God what you need...'
Philippians 4: 6 KJV

I have come to learn of the importance of being committed to prayer and now I have made the whole process habitual within my daily life. Every morning as I awake the first thing that I think about is God and prayer. There are times when I am not in the mood to wake up at 5am or 6am in the morning for a variety of reasons. Being human means that difficult times will come. We can call them test, trails or tribulations but come they may, hard and fast leaving hurt and devastation in their path. However, it is through these times that I often find that I encounter the most barriers to prayer. I feel that through feelings of the flesh I allow the darkness access and I allow myself to be distant from God. Although I know that it is then that I need extra support. I look else where outside of God and the kingdom, and lean on my own understanding, it is very easy to forget. I may not seek his guidance through prayer on a matter without even realising it as it is menial. I often find He still works on situations because he knows my heart.

The Holy Ghost

The Holy Ghost is an important part of our relationship with God as it is through the Holy Ghost that we feel the Father's presence, build a relationship, take correction, understand and hear His Words. Therefore when we pray we ask to first receive the Holy Spirit in order to open up a dialogue with the Lord and begin to communicate in so doing build an effective relationship with Our Lord. In our most intimate moments in prayer whilst the Holy Spirit is moving within us there are tears but a peaceful stillness a calm when we have achieved kenosis: emptied ourselves, in order to receive you have invited the Holy Ghost in and when the Spirit has entered there is now dialogue with the Lord.

But thou, when thou prayest, enter thy closet, and when thou has shut thy door, pray to thy Father which is in secret; and thy Father which seeth in secret shall reward thee openly".
Matthew 6:6 KJV

It is important to learn to wait on the Lord and listen in silence through meditating, prayer, fasting or reading of scripture, there could even be a dream you or someone else has had for you or a word, a telephone call with some news. Be still aware and listen for the response.

'...Be still and know that I am God...' Psalms: 46 KJV

A strong prayer life takes practice, dedication and commitment. Prayer needs to be habitual and you need to practice daily, regularly like Jesus:

'And it came to pass in those days, that he went out into the mountain to pray, and continued all night in prayer.'
Luke 6:12 KJV

The disciple Paul wrote: '...But we will give ourselves continually to prayer, and to the ministry of the word...'
Act 6:4 KJV

We pray for God to move in their life on a particular situation or matter but when we find it seems that he is not listening as we ask and it seems that He does not appear to be answering or in 'our' minds giving. we think we have been forgotten. However must not forget, sometimes, just as children, ask for things that a responsible parent or adult must say no to out of love so does the Father. This happens to us as parents and guardians with our own children in life. The result is the child is often left feeling dejected, upset and hard done by. In that case it is generally agreed that this is because the child is too young to understand the actions performed for their benefit, yet with age will come understanding. That is how I see the things which are denied to me. Maybe it will do me harm instead of good.

'...The Lord disciplines those he loves...'
Hebrews 11:31 KJV

Discipline and love, that is how I describe things that I perceive the Lord does not want for me. My 'old school' Mama would always say in her broad Dominican accent, "Y is a capital letter with a long tail, when you grow you will know", to the majority of my awkward childhood questions that parents dread. I was always inquisitive with a constant stream of questions needing answers. Now as a 'modern day contemporary parent' of two grown children 28 and 24 years old whom are well rounded and know the Lord and generally live a decent standard of life. I can have an understanding for the need of effective communication and breakdown in communication. I would still say that through the growth period labelled as adolescence and puberty young people are not always themselves as there are biological, hormonal and a number of changes which they are experiencing as they leave puberty and enter adulthood. They can display irrational behaviour to say the least. I have realised my parents were right on that note as sometimes children do not have the capacity of life experience, knowledge and maturity to understand, even if it were to be explained. I have come to know this is how the Father works. It is not what we need, maybe he said no or it is not the right time. When we do not receive in our plea for help. Everything in Gods time and as we are imperfect human's and children in Christ we are too young to understand and could never comprehend how His time, will, thought processes are assessed or even quantified. Thus it is pointless to try. Patience is a virtue and although, the Lord said ask and I will answer, seek and you shall find. He did not say you would always like the answer and get what you want. When I ask and it appears that I am not being answered. I know that he might have said no as it is not right for me. It may even just be the wrong time.

Peter therefore was kept in prison; but prayer was made without ceasing of the church unto God for him: This shows the power of collective prayer as a church unified collective and body in the Spirit. Even though he was in prison facing persecution for his belief he still prayed and reached out.

Forgiveness

Peter asked Jesus how many times should he forgive someone who had sinned or trespassed against him. He replied "...Seventy times seven..." Matthew 18:21 KJV

Fundamentally forgiveness is the most important quality, character trait that we as disciples are called to display. Above all else we are all asked to forgive because we as individuals are imperfect human beings. Although it can seem hard and fraught with struggle forgiveness is essential.

'Jesus said when we pray ask for the Lord to forgive us: "...And forgive us our debts, as we also have forgiven our debtors..."' Matthew 6:11-12 KJV

Analyse this statement, Jesus is showing us that once we are followers we can ask to be forgiven and it will be done. It is a part of our agreement which was signed sealed and delivered with the crucifixion of Jesus Christ. Therefore, if we wish to be forgiven daily by the Father we must also display a forgiving nature, soul and heart. That one act of forgiveness can never be underestimated or trivialised. In my understanding it is through this act that all our faith is based. The fact that the Lord sent His only begotten son to live and die so that we may receive His Grace necessary to be reborn in His image. He sacrificed His son and allowed him to take on the sins of the world for us so that we can repent, ask to be forgiven and be reborn through the blood of the innocent lamb that was shed.

Hatred hurts it cuts like a knife and does not come from the Lord, it is the flesh and the material world conflicting. Do not mistake it. To walk around with hate in ones heart for another human being corrupts the soul. The soul becomes redundant consumed and eaten up with thoughts which can be categorised as revenge or pay back. The soul is then in decay being slowly eaten away like a cancer destroying every facet of the heart and all in its path. You have given the Devil access as it is through those negative emotions that he can operate and have control and dominion over your life. Truly give your burdens to Him relieve yourself of those negative emotions and let Him reserve judgement and punishment for your transgressors as there is none swifter, just, right and true like the judgement of the Lord. It is powerful and holy sanctioned.

'...But if ye forgive not men their trespasses, neither will your Father forgive your trespasses.. '
Matthew 6:16 KJV

This is an example of the commandment do unto other in operation here. Jesus is the most effective example of a forgiving soul ever to have lived. When you read from the Old and New Testament the accounts, and biographies of Jesus's life and wondrous works illustrate, terrible things happened to all number of biblical figures from the John the Baptist, The Apostles, Moses to Job. It is always the love of the Lord and doing his will that allows them to complete prophesy overcome and fulfil Gods purpose for each of them. However, Jesus always looked for the good in others. His forgiving and humble nature and attitude is consistent, even at times to his own detriment he exercised forgiveness and love. Bad things occurred such as the conspiracy surrounding his own death and preaching of the words of the Gospels. He is indeed the sacrificial lamb sent by Our Father to purge the world of its inequity and sin and create a line through which we can come to our Lord through use of the Holy Ghost Spirit.

He is the eternal optimist and beacon for hope in the Bible. Whilst even on the cross he remarks:

"...Forgive them as they know not what they do..."
Luke 23:34 KJV

Still knowing that everything is for a reason and prophesy must be fulfilled. All the time acknowledging it is all a part of the masters plan and more importantly Gods will. In this way his presence demonstrates a calm, peace and stillness needed from us all. He shows us how in His numerous encounters to use, feel and be empowered by the grace of the all powerful and knowing being that is God.

Forgiveness, charity, understanding and compassion are qualities which we as followers must strive to obtain. It is written:

"And now abideth faith, hope, charity, these three; but the greatest of these is charity".

Charity is described as the greatest character trait of all as there are times that even in Christ one can feel a little sorry for one's self and fall short of faith and hope but charity, 'do unto others' will always carry you through the pain and support you in your walk to the other side of the sometimes dark tunnel of existence. When I have been hurt in some way I have found it difficult to get over it. However, now I understand the need to walk through the pain and allow myself to feel whatever emotions I need to before it is resolved in Christ. I had to understand that there are always lesson to be learnt in the painful lonely darkness of a tunnel. The lessons will also help and strengthen me. The saying goes if it does not kill me it will make me stronger. Understanding is referred to as more precious than merchandising, silver and gold in the scriptures. A forgiving soul is something we must always seek as it is on that foundation God's love is based. His word is our power I have said it countless times.

Faith

'We walk by faith, not by sight' 2 Corinthians 5:17 KJV

The actual word faith is mentioned 247 times in the Bible: King James Version KJV. Faith is something that you can not see or be without. We as individuals can live in such fear that it can almost seem impossible to step out in faith instead of fear with the wrong influences around one. Bathe yourself in your word it is your shield and buckler. The latter fear, has a safe comfortable home in the constant flesh and spiritual conflict we experience. We are on the battlefield of existence fighting for justice. WE ARE AT WAR!! psychological warfare, with spiritual wickedness and powers, rulers of darkness of this world. It is serious business. Fear insist that you do not try something new or think of the possibilities beyond your circumstances or life background and choices. Fear dictates that you should stay on safe mode and never seek to reach unimaginable horizons that faith can offer.

'...The Lord is my helper, I will not be afraid...'
Hebrews 13:6 KJV

"And Jesus said unto them, because of your unbelief: for verily I say unto you if you have faith as a grain of mustard seed, you shall say unto this mountain, remove hence to yonder place: and it shall remove: and nothing shall be impossible unto you."
Matthew 17:20 KJV

Faith tells you that you can do it and all you need is His help and support He will bring the people you need to support you along the way and fill you with the knowledge, wisdom, skills and abilities and the know needed to achieve the task at hand. He will surround you with people who are for you and not against you. The Lord operates in faith but the Devil operates in fear. When the Lord puts his hand on a situation it almost seems to have a domino effect everything begins to fall into place without much exertion and work. On a regular basis you will find that you constantly have encounters in every sphere of your life which are relevant to your purpose and path. People and situations will arise with ease to help you along your way and Journey.

Faith is formed through belief and conviction in that belief. 1st Corinthians: 9, talks of 'the gift of faith' a greater level of faith the ability to believe God. We must be convinced in Gods ability and the ability of our own faith.

'...And he rose and rebuked the wind and said unto the sea, peace, be still. And then the wind ceased, and there was a great calm. And he said unto them why are ye so fearful? How is it that ye have no faith?' Mark 4:39 KJV

This state of 'being' can be described as 'a blind knowing' that can only be felt in the depth of your Spirit and soul, for me through personal revelation in my life. Through the laws of submission and acknowledgement of that authority we surrender.

'... Thomas, one of the twelve...was not with them when Jesus came...The disciples therefore said unto him, We have seen the Lord. But he said unto them, Except I shall see in his hands the print of the nails, and put my finger into the print of the nails, and thrust my hand into his side, I will not believe...Jesus saith unto him, Thomas, because thou hast seen me, thou hast believed: Blessed are they that have not seen, and yet have believed...'
John 20:24-30 KJV

'So fix our eyes on not what is seen, but what is unseen. For what is seen is temporary but what is unseen is eternal.'
2 Corinthians 4:18 KJV

For me 'blind knowing' was no easy feat I had to question. I now know without the need for the conventional, scientific ideology of physical truth and facts that contemporary society is often driven and governed by. It is my confidence, courage and strength in God that has given me an unshaken belief that there are somethings that can not be explained in this world and are truly indescribable and for me it is not a Unidentified Flying Object UFO or something in the universe. It is Our Lord in all His splendour and magnificent glory. Faith is something I first visualise, vocalise and then I embrace with all of the force and might that I possess in order for advancement. It is at that moment, that juncture faith is realised.

'I am God and there is none else. There is no God beside me.' Isaiah 45:5-6 KJV

Religious belief and faith in that belief could definitely be described as an individual and personal thing in western contemporary society. It has also be asserted that which ever belief one holds is determined by several human factors i.e. culture, race, nationality and background among other factors. I read the Bible but did not allow myself to understand the text and hidden meanings contained as to unlock the secrets I had to build an intimate relationship with God through Christ, habitual prayer and scriptural solidifying. The foundation of my faith and belief in a definite purpose of what as a unique individual I was born to achieve. Forgiveness, charity, understanding and compassion are qualities which we as followers must strive to obtain.

Words

Words

James Allen asserts in his book As a man thinketh first published back in 1902, you literally are what you think.

'Mind is the Master-power that moulds and makes, And Man is Mind, and evermore he takes the tool of thought, and shaping what he wills brings forth a thousand joys, a thousand ills: He thinks in secret, and it comes to pass: Environment is but his looking-glass.' Allen J: As a man thinketh:

Along my journey I have come to believe that the mind is not just an organ but it is the nerve center of the body. The body can operate without the mind to a point but there is no substance i.e. if for any reason the brain has ceased to operate. It needs to be fed and nourished for growth and elevation through re-thinking thoughts processes. It could be argued as being one of the most essential organs of the body as it is vital for the others to work effectively. Thoughts permeate through out our body we must guard our thoughts. A useful way to view this is with the concept of laws of attraction and suggestion. In other words we are whatever we think we are. The capacity for what the mind can do is 'mind blowing', if you will pardon the pun.

'And seek not ye what ye shall eat or what ye shall drink neither be ye of doubtful mind.'
Luke 12:29 KJV

Motives and thoughts can be dangerous. We think it, then we say it and we have spoken those words whatever they may be into our existence. The tongue is a powerful tool, what comes out of the mouth defiles the body.

'...Behold I have put my words in thy mouth...'
Jeremiah:1:9 KJV

It has been said that the pen is mightier than the sword. I have come to realise that my purpose in life is to read, write, teach and preach the word. That can feel like a mammoth task. However, I feel a compulsion and as though I am compelled as a part of what I believe is my purpose and the task that I was put here and created to perform.

Therefore, I gather strength from knowing that, He would never give that which I can not handle. He knows my portion as He has shared it out. The Lord has given us the power to speak positivity into our lives and that of others around us for positive things to come. An abusive husband that tells his victimised battered wife that she is nothing and will never amount to anything without him, is in effect 'washing his mouth' on her and her circumstances. In other words he is speaking negativity into her life. Until she has the faith to believe that he is wrong nothing will change. She needs to believe, then step out on that faith and belief otherwise nothing will change as she now sees the future he has set before her. He had vocalised it she has visualised it. Until she dares to believe that she is worth it and can triumph there will be no improvement in the situation. My mother always said the upholder is worst than the thief. That means the person who stood there and encouraged the individual to thief is worst than the person that actually performed the act of theft.

The stronger that I have become in my Spirit, the closer I have come to Christ the more I understand the need for a follower to be a member of a church. Each of us are a part of one body in Christ described as the schizm in the Bible meaning we are all a part of one body. The declining church membership numbers are often attributed to its lack of relevance in todays world. This is always depicted as a key issue for the modern church. I have spoken to people who would class themselves as Christian but they follow several faiths all rolled up into one thing, their own religion with their own doctrine. There is a big danger of allowing ourselves to be misled into thinking that it is correct and logical to attend, Catholic, Baptist, Anglican or whatever church we feel like attending today as the rationale is that it is all God. Wrong. Apart from the belief in God and Christ as well as certain of the scriptural practices, there are differences in rituals, traditions ceremonies and so on. Each faith has differing beliefs ways of worship, views and opinions. I then often end up with Christians who ask me for my star signs, to determine whether or not our personalities are a match and compatible. Some individuals call themselves followers, without understanding the premise of the Bible as it states that horoscopes are wrong as they predict the future only God does that, its simple.

Music

I believe that a part of my identity has been shaped and influenced by the music which I have listened to growing up. In adulthood musical preferences that I hold are easy to articulate. However, looking back at my musical tastes has been enlightening and elevating as I have explored musics importance as a follower and its meaning to me. I critically analyzed how I use, listen and interpret music and the changes along my journey as I have grown and evolved.

During my teenage years how and what I listened to was restricted because of my upbringing the fact that and Terrestrial Television was all that was available. Television is much different today with the technological advancements of Satellite, Cable and Digital television. There were only three channels with designated slots for Children's Programming, Sports, News etc. The format was largely the same as today, without choice. There were no videos and CD's. I only heard what I considered to be Gospel music at home and in church and they were always traditional hymns. I can not remember when I began to watch Top of the Pops but growing up I was an avid viewer as were all of my peers. The show was created and produced by BBC Television and was a mainstream music chart show. It boasted ratings of a 12 million strong audiences. However, it has been argued that was due to lack of choice and variety in programming. Everyone wanted to be on the show in the audience dancing. Music of Black Origin, MOBO was the music I listened to mostly at home and was played on tape recorders and record players. My friends and peers alike were fans of mainstream groups such as: Police,

Madness and Kate Bush among others. The same thing applied to the radio, the main stations to listen to were Capital Radio, Radio 1 and Radio London.

Ethnic diversity within the British Broadcasting Industry as a whole was lacking and almost non existent. British Broadcasting was totally monopolised and marginalised back then. There were two Reggae slots that most of the black community listened to. These were David Rodigan at 12pm midnight on a Friday he played Jamaican Dancehall music and Tony Williams at 2pm on a Sunday afternoon he hosted a family show. This show had more of a Black British influence with a Jamaican Reggae fusion called 'Lovers Rock'. He focused on promoting music from black British acts. It was referred to as the 'Rice and Peas Show' as you were usually cooking or eating your Sunday dinner which always consisted of Rice and Peas, whilst you listened. By the mid 1980's both shows were axed. In my twenties by the 1990's there was a further shift in representations of MOBO. There was an emergence of illegal Pirate community radio stations. This was directly due to technological advancements. The shift meant transmission equipment needed to rig up a radio station was increasingly affordable and easily accessible. Through the emergence of the Pirate Broadcasting it allowed for more choice in a wider genre of music available to listen to, specifically the American influence.

This now introduced me to Disco, R&B, Culture, Funk, Indie, Rare Grove and Soul. My musical taste in popular music and genres of music had changed. Previously my main influences in popular music were mainly mainstream: Motown, Pop, Rock and Country Western.

Music has many different uses for me and it has always been a form of release and comfort. Some of the music described as 'Worldly Music' which I listened to previously, I still like to hear and enjoy listening to as they hold memories and nostalgia related to my life and past. However, it does not compare to the feelings evoked within me through the power of the Holy Ghost present within Gospel Music as the Lord works through it. The way I listen to music and the meaning created out of the messages being sent through the music is what has changed. The 'Worldly Music' I listened to no longer holds a resonance for me. There are no specific messages operating within it. It is not always self affirming empowering 'Good News' either. I feel that it is important to note that although I love Gospel music I have preferences as to certain genres I prefer and can relate to. Within Gospel music there are 'Sub Genres'. God answered my prayers and showed me that I can listen to my music but he gave me a new way of viewing and understanding the music which I listened to and the words present. He also gave me a new genre of music to listen to as he evolved my enjoyment of music.

Gospel Music

In my opinion the definition of Gospel music, what it is and what it stands for, could be suggested as being mis-understood by many of us. I too had no idea of the immense power of the music, how the Lord wants it to work and the fact that it is another tool that the Lord has bestowed upon us to give him praise and worship, support and enjoyment for us. To quote the Terry Newsome song entitled Soul Music in which he describes Gospel Music as ". Soul Music, music for your soul...inspired by the Holy Ghost". People regularly confuse genre with content.

Gospel music is not about the genre of music. Whether it be a traditional hymn or more contemporary: Hip Hop, Rap, Rock, Jazz, Country and Western or even Indie, it is the words. The words present within the lyrics which are the spread of the gospel through the music. The genre is then just used as a vehicle to deliver the words. The words contained in the book are the armour, power and protection we need to cover us in Christ daily. It is the truth and the light which we seek. We use it and have no idea of what power we control and is present within our mouths and Spirit. We have been given the power to speak over ourselves, lives to change circumstances. Just one measure which quantifies how far I have come in my journey.

In the past I would generally describe myself as a Black British educated woman. But now I know that God power transcends all, from my race, gender or even social class. My existence is no longer solely based on my racial origin qualifications or even gender and culture. It is based on humanity as that is what God teaches, do good and it will come back to you. I no longer denigrate myself to the restrictive categories which the world and man have place upon me. As a Black Woman I was inhibited and restricted at times. However, as a Woman of God which is the role I strive toward, I can achieve anything in His name and by His will. I have been transformed. He has taken me from the pit of despair to the pulpit of glory and given me a new way to view my life and circumstances.

'...I am crucified with Christ:nevertheless I live; yet not I, but Christ liveth in me:and the life which I now live in the flesh I live by the faith of the Son of God, who loved me, and gave himself for me...'
Galatians 2:20 KJV

It is important to stress the importance of fellowship as a part of the body we as disciples can not survive out there alone not belonging to a church to draw strength from. Kingdom business is serious business and we are ALL as followers called to rally round and pray on purpose to ascertain in what fashion, form, style and role we have been assigned to lead others as sheep to the Lord and encourage each others God given gifts and talents for use in His ministry.

Ray Charles had roots in gospel and was influenced by the church, even through his years of drug addiction. That is now widely accepted he is respected for it and is credited as the Man of Soul and cross over music to mainstream. When he first sang in bars and clubs in his early career as depicted in the film Ray, Christians saw it as sacrilege of the Lords music and words. Historically, in the era of the 1930's and 1940's individuals and society was considered to be a lot more God fearing and religious. Ray brought a new style and interpretation of music along with an understanding. That is that the actual genre or style of music is not actually relevant.

It is the message that it brings, contained in the words of the music, the lyrics.

The significance of Ray here is in his day he was one of the first established artist to sing gospel music over music that was viewed as mainstream and worldly. Gospel influenced his music and reached others.

The importance of all this is that many people in today's society are alienated from organised religion and God. I focus on the young because they are tomorrow and the future. However, Just as in Ray Charles day we as adults must understand that the music does not make the song it is the lyrics which are scripture.

Paul in Ephesians 5:19 talks of the need for us all to be:

'Speaking to one another in Psalms and hymns and spiritual songs, singing and making melody in your heart to the Lord'

It is true that King David loved an opportunity for a song and dance in the name of the Lord. David was a Musician and Shepherd before Samuel anointed him and he eventually became King. He penned 73 of the Psalms and one of the most popular and most recited is the 23rd Psalm: The Lord is my shepherd. He knew that there is always time for joy, thanks giving and worship. I must confess I loved a rave in my younger days. Music is another way to connect with the lost souls for them to receive the healing and salvation we have come to know as followers. I believe that we need to find more effective ways to reach out to people and help them to find new and improved ways to learn, discuss and form an understanding of the gospel and God. I harness Gods power by keeping his words on my lips and in my heart and mind daily. Davids relationship with God and his character show the importance of music in the Kingdom but not as a diversion as a tool for the Lords word.

Musicians have always been important in the Bible. They were the Levites and priest who were sanctified were chosen as the musicians in the Old Testament. It was the musicians that were sent out first. Historically in war the trumpeters are always sent out first to sound the trumpet to commence the war and begin the advance and attack. Additionally the drummers keep the pace for everyone to follow. When the Walls of Jericho came falling down it was heralded with the sound of trumpets.

'...So the people shouted when the priests blew with the trumpets and it came to pass, when the people heard the sound of the trumpet, and the people shouted with a great shout, that the wall fell down flat...'
Hebrews 11:30 KJV

'...The Levites which were the singers...Being arrayed in white linen, having cymbals and psalteries and harps, stood at the east end of the altar, and with them an hundred and twenty priests sounding with trumpets: It came even to pass, as the trumpeters and singers were as one, to make one sound to be heard in praising and thanking the Lord; and when they lifted up their voice with the trumpets and cymbals and instruments of musick, and praised the Lord, saying, For he is good; for his mercy endureth for ever...'
1 Corinthian 5:12 KJV

Music is a creative art form which allows for self expression. Thus encouraging individuals to express themselves through differing genres advocates and promotes positivity and intern draws them closer to the Gospel. Music has always been an effective medium for reaching out to others and forcing people to take note. It has been used to support political activism, charities, World Peace to freedom of political prisoners. Therefore we need to support Gospel music and the people coming up in the industry as new artist carrying out their purpose and spreading of the word. In 1 Peter, he states:

'For you were sheep going astray but now have returned to the shepherd and Bishop of your souls.'
1 Peter 2:21 KJV

As an adult before I returned to Christ, Gospel music was something I would rarely listen to it would usually be dictated by the occasions such as christenings, weddings or funerals, basically these were the only times which I attended church. However, when I joined my second church there was a Christian couple I met whose ministry was to spread the word through Gospel music. After service one day the wife Sandra approached me and explained that their ministry was to create CD's for new believers to support them in their walk. She asked me what music I listen to and said R&B, Rare Groove, Reggae, Motown and Culture. The following week at church she handed me about 10 CD's. I took them home and began to listen to them. I then realised that I can listen to the genre of music which I liked but it was Gospel music. This opened me up to a whole new world of the Christian Network and Industries. The Lord will always provide. Whilst addressing Christian Life in Colossians 16

'...Let the word of Christ dwell in you richly in all wisdom; Teaching and admonishing one another in Psalm and hymns and spiritual songs. Singing grace in your hearts to the Lord.' Colossians 3:16

The more I applied myself I became more spiritually aware. I began to listened to Gospel artist like Ramaya, Karen Clark and Kierra Sheard, Donnie McClurkin, Dave Hollister originally in the R&B group from the 1990's Black Street, Damita and Deitrick Haddon, Yolanda Adams, Cece Williams, radio stations UCB Gospel and Premier Radio, motivational Evangelist and Preachers like Joyce Meyer, TD Jakes, Chuck Swindoll, Jarrett Cooper, John Hagee among others. I began to watch Bobby Jones Gospel Show as well as shows like Sunday Best this is a Gospel version of the X Factor show. I feel that the Lord showed me that I could still have a love for music in the Kingdom and it could be used to further my journey and walk. Through the Gospel music I have listened to I have learnt many scriptures through the lyrics in the songs which are scripture, prayers and songs of worship from the Psalms. It was not until I began to read the Bible that I became aware that I had learnt scripture through learning the songs. One of my constant issues in my earlier walk was not being able to memorise scripture. I knew certain verses were there but I did not remember where. Due to technology the Bible has become so much more accessible to the mass. It is available on Internet, Apps on Mobiles and Tablets etc. Therefore, I utilise it and I have the Bible on all of my devices, including the audio version. It is always important to read about the current issues and debates surrounding the Bible for clarity and understanding. However, it is imperative not to get caught up in everyone else's understanding and negate the fact that the source is always the Bible and ask God for your understanding and confirmation of that understanding. For me it is all about learning to live differently. I think of it as a lifestyle change from an unhealthy diet to a more healthy one. It is life long change that I am seeking to receive not temporal change as that never helped anyone.

Stand on the 'Word'

Many believers in today's contemporary society speak of "standing on the word". I must confess I to was one that would reel off platitudes such as this, not really understanding the meaning of such a statement. Through my journey and walk I have come realise to stand on the word, I must first know the word, which I am standing on. How is this achieved? Select scriptures which apply to the circumstance or situation and memorise it, pray on it continually. Through life we must study the word laid bear in the Bible. Strip it down, make sense of it, discuss it, relate it to our everyday lives. Live in it habitually, run to the word for guidance and solutions about our issue as we pray. Then wait, watch and listen for the answer. It can come in numerous forms but if we are not vigilant we will miss it without realising. I went to church for years, However, I was not confident to declare it in public forums that I was a believer as I knew I may be called into question. To answer a barrage of enquiring questions which I myself did not know or even think of. Thus I would keep silent. But after beginning to read the word. I found that after I had consumed, digested and made sense of what I had read linked to prayer, I finally began to understand the profound nature of the Bible its place in society and its words as I prayed for wisdom, knowledge and understanding. This has taken years and as we are born of the world, like an addict we must take each day one at a time. Additionally when life pulls us away from God we must run back.

In search of self, the meaning to life and my purpose, I have obviously been led to the age old question of: Why are we here? Many scientist and numerous scholars have not found the conclusive answer as yet. For me unless you consider Christ and God, there is no purpose. Living in this world I hold the theory that there is the existence of two opposing universes operating on two different fields and atmospheres yet intertwining in our modern everyday life. I describe them as the material and the spiritual plains but the latter is often unseen. We all hold a Spirit which is linked to our soul, who we are? this filters through to the core of our being and it extends to the utmost depths of ourselves. The core of who and what we are with NO FRILLS. The predominant theme in most religious philosophy is love always, Love thy neighbour as yourself. There are also rights, wrongs, ritual, traditions, morals and values.

There was a time when I struggled with my writing after having studied, I worked on perfecting my style of writing, it began to change from highly political and emotive to spiritual and searching after I was saved and baptized. I would write a piece of creative writing such as a poem and there He was, somehow God, scripture or spiritual reference would pop up in a verse or a reference to Him. The struggle was that I loved the Lord but I did not combine, ambition, purpose and gift. Writing for me is a career and my bread and butter. Consequently, I before I first published did not believe that someone would want to read my words and that there was not really a market for the spiritual writings genre as oppose to the mainstream market. I would pray about the situation, read my Bible and fellowship attend church and attempt to walk in the Spirit checking in on the Lord at all times. Here I was on one of the most significant journeys in my life a journey into myself where I would have to unlearn ideas, habits and a general sense of being which I had held for a lifetime. My strict upbringing and discipline in the church that I believe made me become disenchanted with religion that had shaped my earlier life and become an agnostic, had shaped me to comeback. I knew God but I did not have an actual intimate relationship with God. I read scripture everyday yet I did not have a good knowledge and lack of understanding of the scripture we lived by when I was a child. I would even say at times in my life on my journey and search I have allowed others through difficult times to make me question the existence, of Our Father. God forgive me.

As my faith grew, I began to surrender myself to His authority. The more I attempted to walk in the Spirit more was revealed to me he began to prepare me and I was being obedient not always willingly, sometime kicking and screaming ever so silently. One thing is sure I never gave up or lost sight of what I believed in and what I felt that the Lord had shaped me to do, teach and write touching lives and reaching people in need spreading the gospel of love.

In the Kingdom today just as in the Bible there are many jobs, roles, talents, gifts, skills and purposes. Everyone is important in church from the cleaner to Pastors, Elders, Administration, and the Congregation. Churches are registered as businesses or they could not survive. The world and flesh place a heirachy of importance of positions. I believe that the Bible shows us that we are all important and so is our assignments in His Kingdom.

'...There are difference of administration but the same Lord...'
1 Corinthians 12:4 KJV

When my time is done all I want is to be in is the Eternal Kingdom. I may not be the most important as I am flesh and born of sin so in constant conflict and struggle with the Spirit and flesh. However, I will be content to be the least, so long as I am allowed to enter into the Pearly Gates I will be content with my life when I give my final account when the roll is called. Read, study, fellowship with one another, pray and build an intimate honest relationship with God and watch your life transform. Once you apply yourself to the word and God touches your life, it will never be the same. Bible study has strengthened my walk being, journey and more importantly purpose that the Lord created me for. That is to teach, write, speak and support others to strengthen, change and improve their lives.

About the Author

Augustina born and bread in Newham, East London is the founder of Kreative Educational Solutions and KESPublishing. She is an Author of a variety of genres and a Poet. She holds a BA Honours in Communication Studies and a PGCE and she writes under the pseudo name of Nubian-Tee. Augustina has a zeal for promoting and encouraging the enjoyment of reading and writing for pleasure in order to raise literacy standards in our communities. She sponsors several free creative writing workshops and unpublished writers through her organisation in deprived or urban inner city areas in London. Augustina has been writing for years and is an educationalist with a passion. My Journey is her debut book. She is an Educational Consultant, Teacher and Motivational Speaker. Through her work she is able to empower individuals supporting them to better their lives and life chances through education both informal, formal and through utilising life experience.

Shaleta Grant

Background to My Journey

I have endeavoured to bring to you the 'truth' as I know it to have been delivered to me through the Spirit, study and application of scripture. Writing this book has given me no end of conflict and struggle as I attempted to uncover key issues and debates surrounding my faith, scars and flaws laid bare and the Bible. I believe that the Bible is the inspired word of God. Therefore I was very aware of being careful to observe my journey and the messages the Lord has delivered to me in an honest manner. I could be described as a scholar and an academic with a good grasp of the literary form. I am an English teacher, publisher and author. However, those skills did not make writing this book easy as one would have expected. It was the content which I struggled with, everything every issues and word was questioned and prayed over. There was then a wait for continual conformation in a dream or a God encounter before I could proceed and move forward on all of the issues, key debate and discourse which surrounds my walk. In order to make an honest sense of my walk. It quickly became evident that it would be impossible to write everything needed within one book. I soon discovered the need for a second book to complete my story. In order to effectively access and understand my walk I needed to lay the foundations in this book. This book began as a joint venture with my friend and fellow writer. However, unexpectedly at the last moment the Lord showed me they needed to be separated into two books and my story needed to stand alone. Be daring step out in faith on Gods word. You must be bold for faith to grow. Abraham was a great man of faith read Romans Chapter four. Believe in God. Faith comes by hearing Gods word. Read the Bible and books around the subjects within for clarity and to find your own way. Check it do not be relaxed in a false sense of security of relying on your pastor. He can bring you to the water but he can not force you to drink of the water. That my fellow sisters and brothers is up to you. Read it then exercise and use the 'Word' and start truly trusting in Him you will grow supernaturally in your spirituality by using and application of biblical knowledge.

The contents of this book has been taken from my life thus it has been sourced from my own life experiences, my loves, hurts, triumphs and ultimate saving in Christ. When I first returned to faith, I needed to read a book like this. It would have made my journey easier and simpler. However, as we all know with God everything happens for a reason at a specific time in the Kingdom. Consequently, if I knew then what I know now, how then would I have brought this book to life in this fashion at this time. I have come a very, long, long way in my walk and life. Through my transformation and continual change one of the most difficulties I have encountered is acceptance. Being accepted by family and 'worldly friends' who are not followers or even spiritual, for that matter. I have found that it is hard for them to treat me differently as they were accustomed to who I was in the world and still appear to be as to all intense and purposes I look the same physically. I had to view the situation as not personal and know that in their eyes they question the authenticity of a sinner like me being saved. Now I was never a really 'bad person' in the great scheme of things. However, in my past I have come from a life of benefits, theft, addiction, cleaner, care giver to cook. I explore this aspect of my life further and in more detail in the second part of this book entitled:'Scars and Flaws'. It is a frank and honest story of Gods audacious power to transform. Through personal revelation, I am my testimony, Why do I believe that God is real? Because I know my life and the fact that he has taken me from the pit of despair to the pulpit of glory. "The Lord works in mysterious ways with wonders to perform", as Mama would always say. He knew that a sinner like me needed gritty personal revelation as testimony and evidence of his truth.

I could be described as someone who is a hard worker, passionate, determined and a joker a kind of no nonsense type of person. I have always been fair and stood against injustice, I have always fought for people being unfairly treated, I am loyal, helpful and supportive to others as I have always endeavoured to treat people the same way that I would like to have been treated. However, it never worked. At times I would go out of my way to help someone and they would always seem to be ungrateful. I would then get upset. Those days are over as I do everything for the love of the Lord and his blessings. If there is something considered a favour that is asked of me. I simply say no if in my heart I do no want to do it. To me it would be a wasted exercise as the Lord knows my heart and will not bless me for that. In so doing I ensure that I rarely look for mans award, just the Lords reward.

'And whatsoever ye do, do it heartily, as the Lord and not unto men...Knowing that of the Lord ye shall receive the reward of the inheritance for ye serve the Lord Christ..'
Colossians 3:23-24

I have learnt that God makes everything meant for negative and bad in our lives turn out for good when He touches the situation and we have the faith to believe and trust in Him. Reading and studying the Bible has cemented my entrance. It is impossible to be a follower without knowledge of the rules to which order you follow, that is a simple logical principle in life. The importance of the Bible can not be stressed negated or undermined. Our old school parents had that down. I am proud to call myself God fearing it is a state which I have sort and obtained with diligence and commitment. I have come to understand and love my mother even more in death than I did in life and I did not think that could be possible but remember He makes the impossible possible and unreal real to us everyday.

My professional and personal life have both showed me that reflection is a necessary state I need to visit regularly. It is upon reflection that we all learn the most effectively. Upon reflection we can critically analyse and learn from our less favourable experiences. I have gained an immense amount of knowledge, wisdom and understanding through writing, research and study for this book. This is my story warts and all. I am certainly not ever nor would I wish to be described as 'perfect'. I am a work in progress, I am a follower of Christ following my Father being God's teaching. I ran from organised religion for years as it always felt judgemental and restrictive and as though I did not belong or fit. I have learnt that in Christ we all fit regardless of age, gender, race, disability or even sexual orientation. I once listened to a visiting powerful pastor and his wife speak at my church named Mike and Sarah Vickers and they explained the issue as simply as this. Christ was sent to correct what happened to Adam and Eve. He came to reverse the curse obtained in the Garden of Eden, the original sin. All that Adam exhorted he came to reverse. Many people preach and misunderstand the concept of the cross. They believe that he went to the cross so that we would not have to. They asserted that this is incorrect. We must one and all pick up the cross daily as we move around in our everyday life. In order to take our Soul to the cross. We must be Spirit led and not Soul led as the Soul is operated by the mind and thus open to corruption like a virtual virus, if it is not monitored by the Spirit. True son's and daughters are led by the Spirit of God read Romans 8.

'The Soul is the mind,'
John 10 KJV.

He came to give us a way to receive salvation from the Father He came to teach us repentance and forgiveness and to strive to be better people who love others and do not war. He is a jealous God and He wants us to love only Him which I believe is quite reasonable. We have been given the Holy Ghost Spirit which allows for us to actually communicate and build an intimate relationship with Him. We are called to fulfil His Purpose for which we were all created. I want people to know of His great love for us all and the grace which I have received. I am certainly never described as an individual who looks likes a stereotypical, archetypal, typical Christian or even Evangelist. However, when I speak in the spirit I know that the Lord is using me. Too much has happened to me, I have achieved too much in my life to be arrogant enough to say I did it alone. I have asked and honestly He has answered many many times. When I speak it is people that show me my knowledge as they ask am I a Preacher or an Evangelist and I always say no, even though I am flattered. I am just an ordinary person who loves God and has been transformed through his grace and love and everyone can have that as He has taught me that every single one of us are special yet different in His kingdom. Gods rules and law are not dictated by man and his heirachy. God has His own order in which he can even give a murderer salvation and we will never truly understand.

'But the natural man receiveth not the things of the Spirit of God: For they are foolishness unto him:neither can he know them, because they are spiritually discerned. But he that is spiritual judgeth all things, yet he himself is judged of no man. For who hath known the mind of the Lord, that he may instruct him? But we have the mind of Christ.'
1 Corinthians 2:14 KJV

For it is written:
'My son, keep thy father's commandment, and forsake not the law of thy mother: Bind them continually upon thine heart, and tle them about thy neck. When thou goest, it shall lead thee; when thou sleepest, it shall keep thee; and when thou awakest, it shall talk with thee'
Proverbs 6: 20-22

'Hear, ye children, the instruction of a father, and attend to know understanding. For I give you good doctrine, forsake ye not my law...'
Proverbs 4: 1-2

'My son, attend to my words; incline thine ear unto my sayings. Let them not depart from thine eyes; keep them in the midst of thine heart. For they are life unto those that find them, and health to all their flesh. Keep thy heart with all diligence; out of it are the issues of life.'
Proverbs 4:20-23

I leave you with some quotes on the importance of Bible reading and purposeful living for us all to take direction, nourishment and learning from respected figures from history including broadcasting.

"There is no doubt in my mind that King James Bible and not Shakespeare set this language on its path to become a universal language on a scale unprecedented before or since"
Melvin Bragg

"If you have no – Bible you have no way to live."
Rosa Parks

"There are more sure marks of authenticity in the Bible than in any profane history."
Sir Isaac Newton

"Bible reading is an education in itself."
Lord Tennyson

'Success is a journey and not a destination: it's about discovering your ultimate purpose and pursuing it with everything you have and everything you do'.
Napoleon Hill

Adoration
"Hallowed Be Thy Name"

"Our Father, which art in Heaven
Hallowed be thy Name
Bless the Lord
O My Soul and all that is within me
Bless Your Holy Name
I adore You and make known to You
My adoration and Love this day."
Elohim: The Creator
El-Shaddai: The God Almighty of Blessings
Adonai: My Lord and My Master
Jehovah-Jireh: My Provider
Jehovah-Rapha: My Healer
Jehovah-M'Kaddesh: My Sanctifier
Jehovah-Nissi: My Victory, Banner, and Standard
Jehovah-Shalom: My Peace
Jehovah-Tsidkenu: My Righteousness
Jehovah-Rohi: My Shepherd
Jehovah-Shammah:My Comforter
El-Elyon: The Most Highest Sovereign of the Heavens and Earth

Father your name is Above All Names, Your Word is Law and good. Bless all who believes in you and follows Your Word.

Useful Scripture References:

Matthew	6:9	Songs of Solomon	2:4
Psalm	103:1	Isaiah	59:19
Genesis	1:1-2	Judges	6:24
Psalm	8:5b	Philippians	4:7
Genesis	49	Jeremiah	23:5-6
Genesis	15	2 Corinthians	5:21
Hebrews	13:8	Psalm	23:1

KESPublishing Publications
Presents
Poetic Voices
Voices From The Community

This book is a collection of real empowering, immensely moving and inspiring contemporary poetry. It has mass appeal and has something for everyone and age. It is written by a cooperative of writers and documents the reality of the issues faced in their everyday ordinary lives. The book was produced as a part of a community writing experience. Supporting this book, you are not just obtaining a book to read, you are sponsoring FREE community creative writing courses, education and the unemployed into employment In deprived urban inner city areas. through your participation in this writing experience.

Future KESPublishing Publications
The Sequel
Coming Soon

Scars and Flaws

This sequel to My Journey discusses all of the issues involved in living ones life for a purpose with meaning and the ideology that emerges out of redirecting the mind and controlling one's thought processes. It is a gritty look at my actual life and my life experiences. My Journey sets the stage for an identification of where my values and ideologies about life derive. Scars and Flaws is an autobiographical story which explores my life before God. It Begins where My Journey ends.

E : Book and Paperback available from KES and Amazon Websites.
E : as@kespublishing.co.uk
W: http://kespublishing.co.uk
W: http://kreativeducationalsolutions.co.uk
M: 079506437221

Made in the USA
Charleston, SC
21 May 2015